A GARDEN OF PRAYER

A GARDEN OF PRAYER

A Family Treasury

Illustrated by JULIE RAUER

Edited by JENNA BASSIN and JANE LAHR

A Jane Lahr Enterprise

PHILOSOPHICAL LIBRARY

New York

God and Father of us all...Direct those who in
this our generation speak where many listen,
who write what many read, and who show
what many see, that they may do their part in
making the heart of our people wise, its mind
sound, and its will righteous.

David B. Collins, 20th century

Library of Congress Cataloging-in Publication Data

A Garden of prayer

  1. Prayers. I. Bassin, Jenna, 1945-
II. Lahr, Jane.
BV245.G36 1988   242'.8   88-25566
ISBN 0-8022-2551-1

Copyright 1989 by Allied Books, Inc.
31 West 21st Street, New York, New York, 10010

PREFACE

In the months we spent gathering the prayers for this book, it seemed to us that they organized themselves into an emotional, spiritual, and chronological cycle closely resembling that of a garden transformed by the eternal cycle of the seasons. Thus our title, *A Garden of Prayer*.

Each of the five sections is named for one of the seasons, including a second spring of rebirth. The book opens with the ebulliantly youthful prayers of Spring—full of hope, celebration and yearning. The prayers of Summer are those of the adult in full bloom, immersed in the concerns of family, relationship, and work. Autumn follows with the muted voice of growing maturity that begins to question itself on deeper levels, seeking to better understand the changes life brings. In the prayers of Winter we confront profound issues of identity, the condition of our faith and our mortality. Finally, with the Returning Spring come prayers of renewal. Greater depths of understanding and renewed faith lead us to see our loved ones and friends, our community, our nation, and the entire planet in the clear light of affirmation and caring.

This is truly a book for each member of the family, honoring each rite of passage, each season of life.

We were personally inspired by the extraordinary variety of voices that became part of our prayer cycle: St. Francis of Assisi, King David, Robert Louis Stevenson, an anonymous African girl, Thomas Merton and St. Thomas Aquinas, Abraham Lincoln, Dag Hammarskjöld, Teilhard de Chardin, Carmen de Gasztold, Beethoven, an aging medieval woman, Mustafah the tailor, a hermit. Each voice is an integral part of the whole, complementing, harmonizing, and supporting each other in one extended, vibrant expression of celebration and reverence.

In preparing *A Garden of Prayer*, we spent a great deal of time reading each section aloud. We suggest you do the same for we discovered that sharing the book in this way is deeply rewarding. Try it in family groups or with friends, each section separately, or, even better, read the entire cycle from beginning to end. The myriad voices, nations, and cultures blend into a melodic whole that we hope will bring with it courage, grace and transcendence.

Jenna Bassin and Jane Lahr

CONTENTS

SPRING

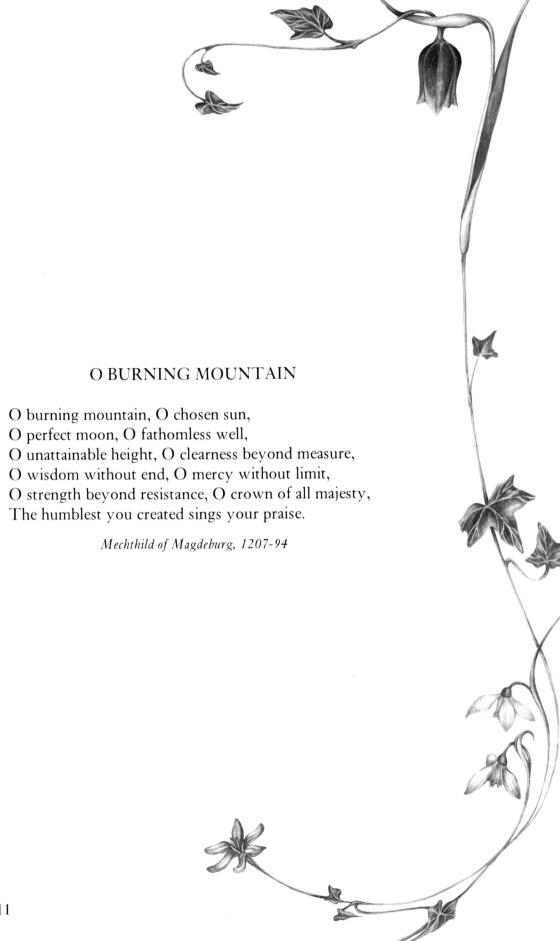

O BURNING MOUNTAIN

O burning mountain, O chosen sun,
O perfect moon, O fathomless well,
O unattainable height, O clearness beyond measure,
O wisdom without end, O mercy without limit,
O strength beyond resistance, O crown of all majesty,
The humblest you created sings your praise.

Mechthild of Magdeburg, 1207-94

PRAYER OF THE BUTTERFLY

Lord!
Where was I?
Oh yes! This flower, this sun,
thank you! Your world is beautiful!
This scent of roses. . .
Where was I?
A drop of dew
rolls to sparkle in a lily's heart.
I have to go. . .
Where? I do not know!
The wind has painted fancies
on my wings.
Fancies...
Where was I?
Oh yes! Lord,
I had something to tell you:
Amen.

Carmen Bernos de Gasztold,
20th century

PSALM 150

O Praise God in his holiness:
praise him in the firmament of his power,
praise him in his noble acts,
praise him according to his excellent greatness,
praise him in the sound of the trumpet,
praise him upon the lute and harp,
praise him in the cymbals and dances,
praise him upon the strings and pipe,
praise him on the well-tuned cymbals,
praise him upon the loud cymbals.
Let everything that hath breath praise the Lord!

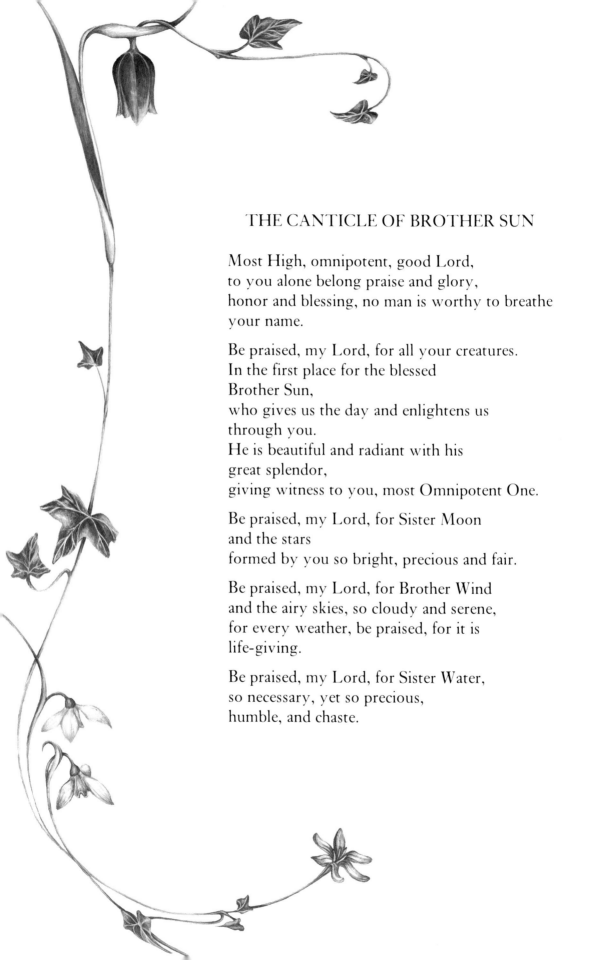

THE CANTICLE OF BROTHER SUN

Most High, omnipotent, good Lord,
to you alone belong praise and glory,
honor and blessing, no man is worthy to breathe
your name.

Be praised, my Lord, for all your creatures.
In the first place for the blessed
Brother Sun,
who gives us the day and enlightens us
through you.
He is beautiful and radiant with his
great splendor,
giving witness to you, most Omnipotent One.

Be praised, my Lord, for Sister Moon
and the stars
formed by you so bright, precious and fair.

Be praised, my Lord, for Brother Wind
and the airy skies, so cloudy and serene,
for every weather, be praised, for it is
life-giving.

Be praised, my Lord, for Sister Water,
so necessary, yet so precious,
humble, and chaste.

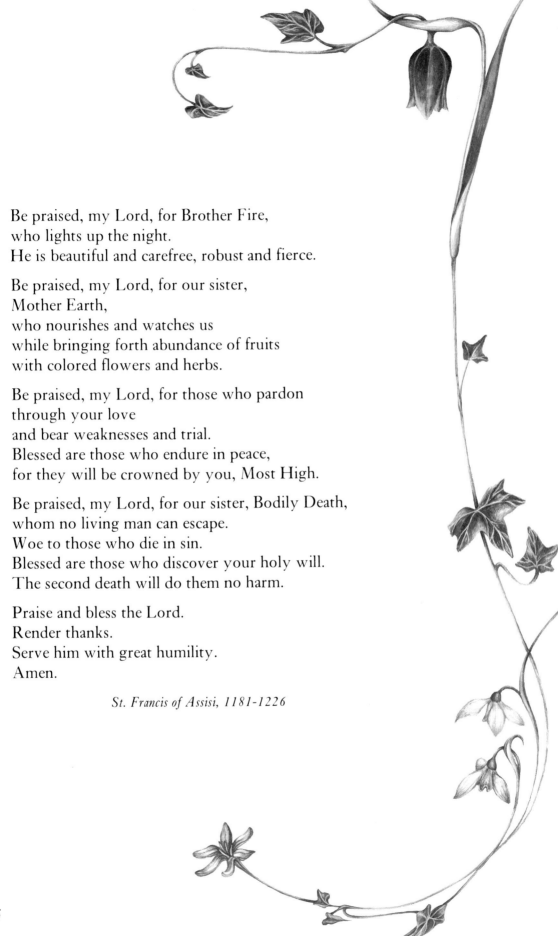

Be praised, my Lord, for Brother Fire,
who lights up the night.
He is beautiful and carefree, robust and fierce.

Be praised, my Lord, for our sister,
Mother Earth,
who nourishes and watches us
while bringing forth abundance of fruits
with colored flowers and herbs.

Be praised, my Lord, for those who pardon
through your love
and bear weaknesses and trial.
Blessed are those who endure in peace,
for they will be crowned by you, Most High.

Be praised, my Lord, for our sister, Bodily Death,
whom no living man can escape.
Woe to those who die in sin.
Blessed are those who discover your holy will.
The second death will do them no harm.

Praise and bless the Lord.
Render thanks.
Serve him with great humility.
Amen.

St. Francis of Assisi, 1181-1226

NATIVE AMERICAN PRAYER

O Great Spirit, whose voice I hear in the winds,
and whose breath gives life to all the world, hear me.
I am small and weak. I need your strength and wisdom.

Let me walk in beauty and make my eyes ever behold
the red and purple sunset.

Make my hands respect the things you have made.

Make my ears sharp to hear your voice.

Make me wise so that I may understand
the things you have taught your people.

Let me learn the lessons you have hidden
in every leaf and rock.

I seek strength, not to be greater than my brother,
but to fight my greatest enemy—myself.

Make me always ready to come to you
with clean hands and straight eyes.

So when life fades, as the fading sunset,
my spirit may come to you without shame.

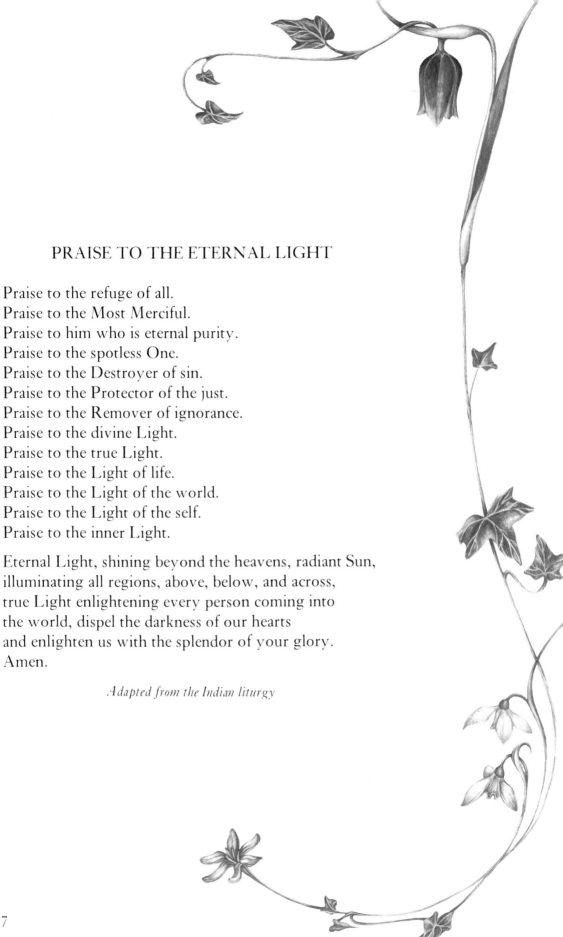

PRAISE TO THE ETERNAL LIGHT

Praise to the refuge of all.
Praise to the Most Merciful.
Praise to him who is eternal purity.
Praise to the spotless One.
Praise to the Destroyer of sin.
Praise to the Protector of the just.
Praise to the Remover of ignorance.
Praise to the divine Light.
Praise to the true Light.
Praise to the Light of life.
Praise to the Light of the world.
Praise to the Light of the self.
Praise to the inner Light.

Eternal Light, shining beyond the heavens, radiant Sun,
illuminating all regions, above, below, and across,
true Light enlightening every person coming into
the world, dispel the darkness of our hearts
and enlighten us with the splendor of your glory.
Amen.

Adapted from the Indian liturgy

PSALM 104

Bless the Lord, my soul.
Lord, my God, how great you are!
Clothed in majesty and glory,
wrapped in a robe of light!

You stretch the heavens out like a tent,
you build your palace on the waters above;
using the clouds as your chariot,
you advance on the wings of the wind;
you use the winds as messengers
and fiery flames as servants.

You fixed the earth on its foundations,
unshakable for ever and ever;
you wrapped it with the deep as with a robe,
the waters overtopping the mountains.

At your reproof the waters took to flight,
they fled at the sound of your thunder,
cascading over the mountains, into the valleys,
down to the reservoir you made for them;
you imposed the limits they must never cross again,
or they would once more flood the land.

You set springs gushing in ravines,
running down between the mountains,
supplying water for wild animals,
attracting the thirsty wild donkeys;
near there the birds of the air make their nests
and sing among the branches.

From your palace you water the uplands
until the ground has had all that your heavens
have to offer;
you make fresh grass grow for cattle
and those plants made use of by man,
for them to get food from the soil:
wine to make them cheerful,
oil to make them happy
and bread to make them strong.

The trees of the Lord get rain enough,
those cedars of Lebanon he planted;
here the little birds build their nest
and, on the highest branches, the stork has its home.
For the wild goats there are the mountains,
in the crags rock badgers hide.

You made the moon to tell the seasons,
the sun knows when to set:
you bring darkness on, night falls,
all the forest animals come out:
savage lions roaring for their prey,
claiming their food from God.

The sun rises, they retire,
going back to lie down in their lairs,
and man goes out to work,
and to labor until dusk.
Lord, what variety you have created,
arranging everything so wisely!
Earth is completely full of things you have made:

among them vast expanse of ocean,
teeming with countless creatures,
creatures large and small,
with the ships going to and fro
and Leviathan whom you made to amuse you.

All creatures depend on you
to feed them throughout the year;
you provide the food they eat,
with generous hand you satisfy their hunger.

You turn your face away, they suffer,
you stop their breath, they die
and revert to dust.
You give breath, fresh life begins,
you keep renewing the world.

Glory for ever to the Lord!
May the Lord find joy in what he creates,
at whose glance the earth trembles,
at whose touch the mountains smoke!

I mean to sing to the Lord all my life,
I mean to play for my God as long as I live.
May these reflections of mine give him pleasure,
as much as the Lord gives me!
May sinners vanish from the earth
and the wicked exist no more!

Bless the Lord, my soul.

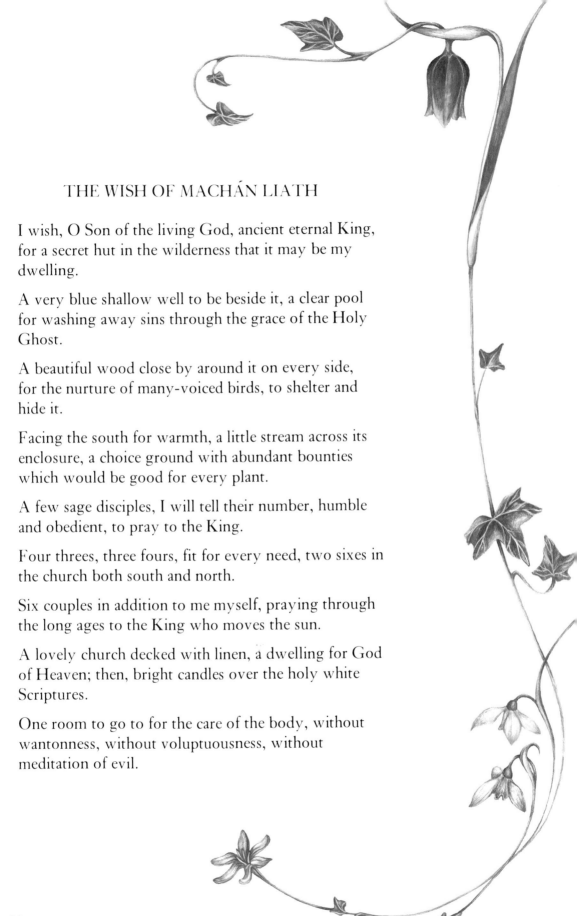

THE WISH OF MACHÁN LIATH

I wish, O Son of the living God, ancient eternal King, for a secret hut in the wilderness that it may be my dwelling.

A very blue shallow well to be beside it, a clear pool for washing away sins through the grace of the Holy Ghost.

A beautiful wood close by around it on every side, for the nurture of many-voiced birds, to shelter and hide it.

Facing the south for warmth, a little stream across its enclosure, a choice ground with abundant bounties which would be good for every plant.

A few sage disciples, I will tell their number, humble and obedient, to pray to the King.

Four threes, three fours, fit for every need, two sixes in the church both south and north.

Six couples in addition to me myself, praying through the long ages to the King who moves the sun.

A lovely church decked with linen, a dwelling for God of Heaven; then, bright candles over the holy white Scriptures.

One room to go to for the care of the body, without wantonness, without voluptuousness, without meditation of evil.

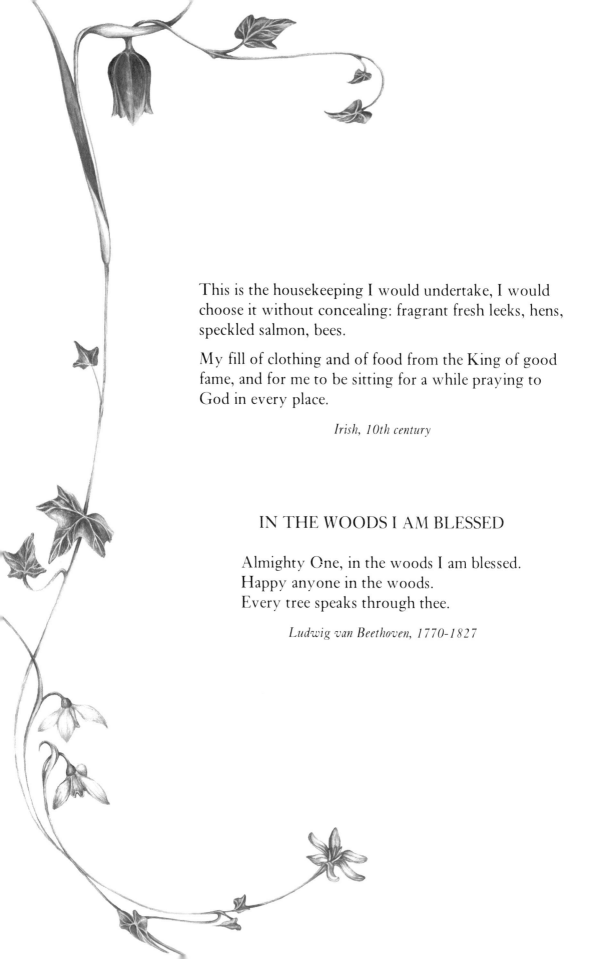

This is the housekeeping I would undertake, I would choose it without concealing: fragrant fresh leeks, hens, speckled salmon, bees.

My fill of clothing and of food from the King of good fame, and for me to be sitting for a while praying to God in every place.

Irish, 10th century

IN THE WOODS I AM BLESSED

Almighty One, in the woods I am blessed.
Happy anyone in the woods.
Every tree speaks through thee.

Ludwig van Beethoven, 1770-1827

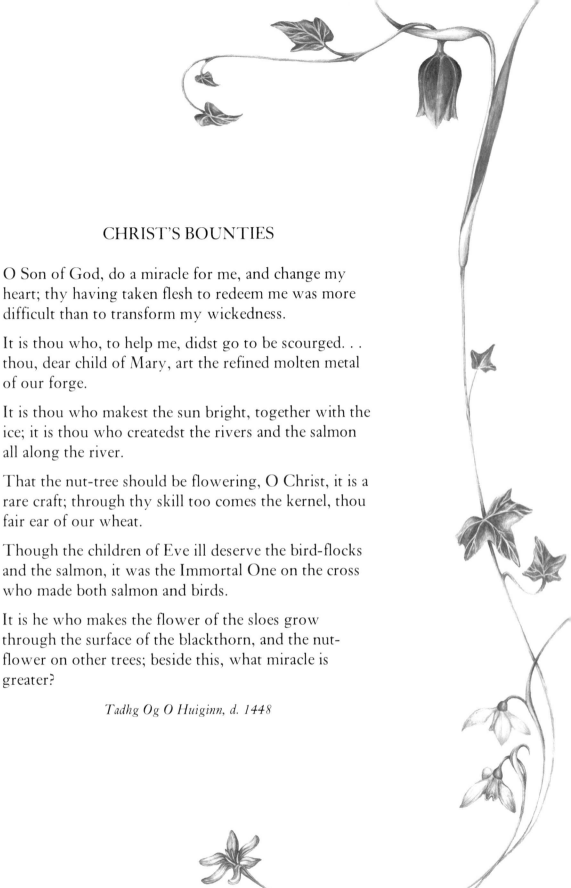

CHRIST'S BOUNTIES

O Son of God, do a miracle for me, and change my heart; thy having taken flesh to redeem me was more difficult than to transform my wickedness.

It is thou who, to help me, didst go to be scourged. . . thou, dear child of Mary, art the refined molten metal of our forge.

It is thou who makest the sun bright, together with the ice; it is thou who createdst the rivers and the salmon all along the river.

That the nut-tree should be flowering, O Christ, it is a rare craft; through thy skill too comes the kernel, thou fair ear of our wheat.

Though the children of Eve ill deserve the bird-flocks and the salmon, it was the Immortal One on the cross who made both salmon and birds.

It is he who makes the flower of the sloes grow through the surface of the blackthorn, and the nut-flower on other trees; beside this, what miracle is greater?

Tadhg Og O Huiginn, d. 1448

FOR ADORATION

For ADORATION seasons change,
And order, truth, and beauty range.
Adjust, attract, and fill:
The grass the polyanthus cheques;
And polish'd porphyry reflects,
By the descending rill.

Rich almonds colour to the prime
For ADORATION; tendrils climb,
and fruit-trees pledge their gems;
And Ivis, with her gorgeous vest,
Builds for her eggs her cunning nest,
And bell-flowers bow their stems.

Now labour his reward receives,
For ADORATION counts his sheaves,
To peace, her bounteous prince;
The nectarine his strong tint imbibes,
And apples of ten thousand tribes,
And quick peculiar quince.

Christopher Smart, 1722-71

WITH ME, LORD

Before I awaken this morning
you are with me, Lord,
and even as I open my eyes
you greet me with the gift of this new day.
May I take this certainty of your presence
with me into all this day can hold.

Be with me now as I go forth—
not as some weird
and ghostly watcher-over-me,
but as a deeper and truer awareness within:

an awareness
which is constantly
opening my mind to ideas,
to possibilities,
to relationships,
to understandings;

an awareness
which is constantly
opening my heart to trust,
to hope,
to sharing and giving,
to the call of the needs
of my fellow-creatures;

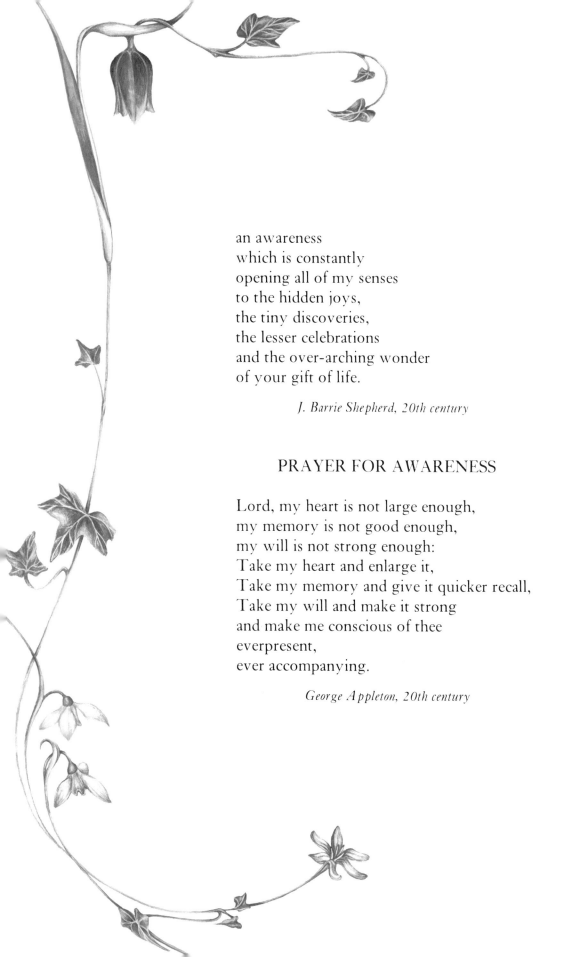

an awareness
which is constantly
opening all of my senses
to the hidden joys,
the tiny discoveries,
the lesser celebrations
and the over-arching wonder
of your gift of life.

J. Barrie Shepherd, 20th century

PRAYER FOR AWARENESS

Lord, my heart is not large enough,
my memory is not good enough,
my will is not strong enough:
Take my heart and enlarge it,
Take my memory and give it quicker recall,
Take my will and make it strong
and make me conscious of thee
everpresent,
ever accompanying.

George Appleton, 20th century

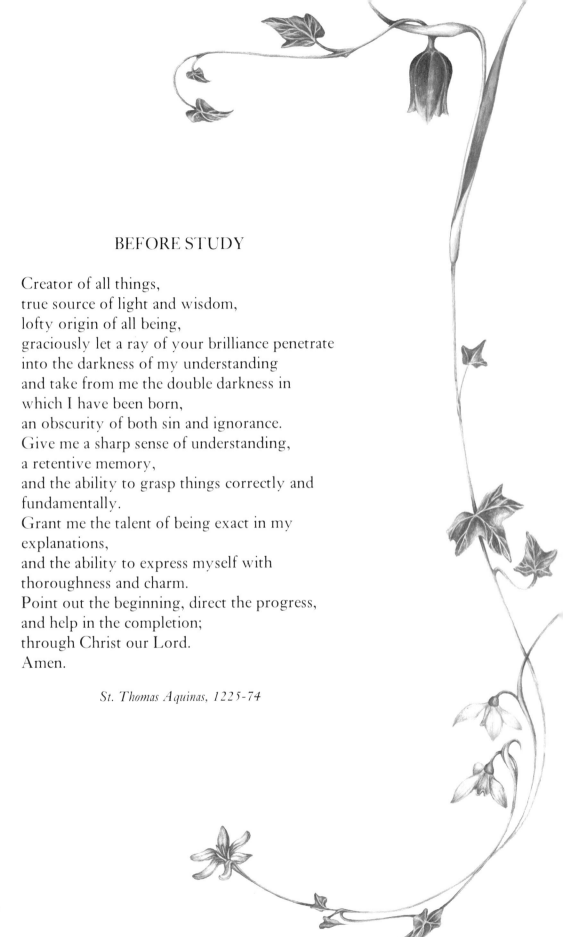

BEFORE STUDY

Creator of all things,
true source of light and wisdom,
lofty origin of all being,
graciously let a ray of your brilliance penetrate
into the darkness of my understanding
and take from me the double darkness in
which I have been born,
an obscurity of both sin and ignorance.
Give me a sharp sense of understanding,
a retentive memory,
and the ability to grasp things correctly and
fundamentally.
Grant me the talent of being exact in my
explanations,
and the ability to express myself with
thoroughness and charm.
Point out the beginning, direct the progress,
and help in the completion;
through Christ our Lord.
Amen.

St. Thomas Aquinas, 1225-74

THINK
THROUGH ME

Holy Spirit think through me
till your ideas are my ideas.

Amy Carmichael, 1868-1951

BLESS MY STUDIES AND ENDEAVORS

O Lord, who hast ordained labour to be the lot of man,
and seest the necessities of all thy creatures,
bless my studies and endeavors;
feed me with food convenient for me;
and if it shall be thy good pleasure to entrust me
with plenty,
give me a compassionate heart,
that I may be ready to relieve the wants of others;
let neither poverty nor riches estrange my heart
from thee,
but assist me with thy grace so to live
that I may die in thy favor,
for the sake of Jesus Christ.

Samuel Johnson, 1709-84

ACCORDING TO THY HEART

Lord, make me according to thy heart.

Brother Lawrence, 1611-91

LIGHT A CANDLE WITHIN
MY HEART

O Great Chief, light a candle within my heart
that I may see what is therein and
sweep the rubbish from thy dwelling place.

Prayer of An African Girl

THRONED IN MY HEART

I find thee throned in my heart,
my Lord Jesus.
It is enough.

I know that thou art throned in heaven.
My heart and heaven are one.

Gaelic, translated by Alistair Maclean

PSALM 19

The heavens declare the glory of God,
the vault of heaven proclaims his handiwork;
day discourses of it to day,
night to night hands on the knowledge.

No utterance at all, no speech,
no sound that anyone can hear;
yet their voice goes out through all the earth,
and their message to the ends of the world.

High above, he pitched a tent for the sun,
who comes out of his pavilion like a bridegroom,
exulting like a hero to run his race.

He has his rising on the edge of heaven,
the end of his course is its furthest edge,
and nothing can escape his heat.

SUMMER

AN AFRICAN CANTICLE

All you *big* things, bless the Lord
Mount Kilimanjaro and Lake Victoria
The Rift Valley and the Serengeti Plain
Fat baobabs and shady mango trees
All eucalyptus and tamarind trees
Bless the Lord
Praise and extol Him for ever and ever.

All you *tiny* things, bless the Lord
Busy black ants and hopping fleas
Wriggling tadpoles and mosquito larvae
Flying locusts and water drops
Pollen dust and tsetse flies
Millet seeds and dried dagaa
Bless the Lord
Praise and extol Him for ever and ever.

Anonymous

EASING PRESSURE

In the heat of this day, Lord,
may I know your cooling presence,
calming my tension, soothing my fears,
bringing into all the pettiness,
all the overwhelming detail,
all the mind-boggling complexity,
the perspective of your simple word of grace:
"Consider the lilies."

In the din and clash of the next few hours, Father,
let me hear your voice,
centering all relationships, all encounters,
all dispute and controversies,
in the challenge:
"Love your neighbor as yourself."

In the push and shove of my work, Lord,
let me feel your hand,
examining all my decisions,
all my dealings, all my hopes and fears,
in the eternal light of:
"Seek first the kingdom of God."

In the traffic jam of my brain, Father,
may I know your wisdom,
reordering all urgencies,
all priorities,
all dreams and ambitions,
under one supreme claim:
"I am the Lord, your God."

Thus may I walk
by the power of your word,
and not my own.

J. Barrie Shepherd, 20th century

BEFORE THE BATTLE
OF EDGEHILL

O Lord,
thou knowest how busy I must be this day;
if I forget thee, do not thou forget me:
for Christ's sake.

General Lord Astley, 1579-1652

MUSTAFAH THE TAILOR

O God, I am Mustafah the tailor
and I work at the shop of Muhammad Ali.
The whole day long I sit
and pull the needle and the thread through the cloth.
O God, you are the needle
and I am the thread.
I am attached to you and I follow you.
When the thread tries to slip away from the needle
it becomes tangled and must be cut
so that it can be put back in the right place.
O God, help me to follow you
wherever you may lead me.
For I am really only Mustafah the tailor,
and I work at the shop of Muhammad Ali
on the great square.

A Muslim's first prayer as a Christian

ON BUILDING A WALL

On building a wall:
I pray thee, Lord, to make my faith as firmly
established as a house built upon a rock, so that neither
rain, flood nor wind can ever destroy it.

On pruning a tree:
I pray thee, Lord, to purge me and take away my selfishness and sinful thoughts, that I may bring forth more fruits of the Spirit.

On tending sheep:
I pray thee, Lord, to protect me from evil and keep me from want, daily carrying me in thine arms like a lamb.

On winnowing grain:
I pray thee, Lord, to winnow away the chaff from my heart and make it like the true wheat, fit to be garnered in thy barn.

On sowing seed:
I pray thee, Lord, to sow the good seed of virtue in my heart, letting it grow by day and night and bring forth a hundredfold.

On writing a book:
I pray thee, Lord, by the precious blood of Jesus, to pay my debt of sin and write my name in heaven, making me free in body and soul.

On planing wood:
I pray thee, Lord, to make me smooth and straight, fit to be a useful vessel, pleasing to the Lord.

On drawing water:
I pray thee, Lord, to give living water to quench my thirst, and wash away the stains from my heart.

Prayer of Chinese Christian men

WHEN OPENING A DOOR

Prayer when opening door:
I pray thee, Lord, to open the door of my heart to receive thee within my heart.

When washing clothes:
I pray thee, Lord, to wash my heart, making me white as snow.

When sweeping floors:
I pray thee, Lord, to sweep away my heart's uncleanness, that my heart may always be pure.

When pouring oil:
I pray thee, Lord, to give me wisdom like the wise virgins who always had oil in their vessels.

When posting a letter:
I pray thee, Lord, to add to me faith upon faith, that I may always have communication with thee.

When lighting lamps:
I pray thee, Lord, to make my deeds excellent like lamps before others, and more, to place thy true light within my heart.

When watering flowers:
I pray thee, Lord, to send down spiritual rain into my heart, to germinate the good seed there.

When boiling water for tea:
I pray thee, Lord, to send down spiritual fire to burn
away the coldness of my heart and that I may always
be hot-hearted in serving thee.

Prayer of Chinese Christian women

DAY BY DAY

Thank you, Lord Jesus Christ,
For all the benefits and blessings
which you have given me,
For all the pains and insults
which you have borne for me.
Merciful Friend, Brother and Redeemer,
May I know you more clearly,
Love you more dearly,
And follow you more nearly,
Day by day.

St. Richard of Chichester, 1197-1253

THE LORD'S PRAYER

'Our Father who art in heaven,
Hallowed be thy name.
Thy kingdom come,
Thy will be done,
On earth as it is in heaven.
Give us this day our daily bread;
And forgive us our debts,
As we also have forgiven our debtors;
And lead us not into temptation,
But deliver us from evil.'

Matthew 6: 9b-13

FAMILY PRAYER

Lord, behold our family here assembled.
We thank you for this place in which we dwell,
for the love that unites us,
for the peace accorded us this day,
for the hope with which we expect the morrow;
for the health, the work, the food and the bright skies
that make our lives delightful;
for our friends in all parts of the earth.

Give us courage and gaiety and the quiet mind.
Spare us to our friends, soften us to our enemies.
Bless us, if it may be, in all our innocent endeavours;
if it may not, give us the strength
to endure that which is to come
that we may be brave in peril,
constant in tribulation, temperate in wrath
and in all changes of fortune
and down to the gates of death,
loyal and loving to one another.
As the clay to the potter
as the windmill to the wind
as children of their sire,
we beseech of you this help and mercy
for Christ's sake.

Robert Louis Stevenson, 1850-94

ON RENEWING A COMMITMENT

ONE: Holy Creator of Love,
     we celebrate and renew our mutual lives
     that are lived as one.
  We reseal, by this holy prayer,
     our commitment to each other
     to a life of shared dreams, thoughts and feelings.
  We ask Your holy help
     so that we may be always awake
     to the needs of each other,
     needs both spoken and unspoken.
  May our two but twin pathways
     lead us to the fullness of life
     and to You.

OTHER: We ask Your divine protection
     from the strong tides of daily troubles
     that tend to pull us apart from each other.
  Shield us from the social sickness of no
     commitment.
  Show us how to rechannel
     the hidden streams of selfishness
     that always threaten to separate us.

Lord, it was said by the ancients
    that from each of us flows a light
    that reaches straight to heaven;
    that when two persons destined to be united
    come together,
    their two streams fuse into a single bright beam
    reaching to heaven
    and giving splendor to all the universe.
We ask that our love for each other
    will shine as a single flame to all.

ONE: We thank You for the gifts of past years
    as we place our hope in the ancient truth
    that whatever is begun here on earth
    will flower to fullness in heaven.
As a sign of our desire to be united,
    today and in the days to follow,
    we join now our glasses as one
    and share a common chalice of our covenant
    with each other and with You,
    our Lord and God.
Amen.

Edward Hays, 20th century

LISTENING TO OUR CHILDREN

It is so easy, O Lord,
to tell our children what they ought to be
or what they ought to do.
We often forget that they are real people,
with real feelings and fears, desires and ambitions.
Rather than seek to understand them,
we attempt to program them,
insisting that they conform to our image,
trying to mold them into replicas of ourselves.
They are at times so lovely,
at times so cantankerous,
but they are your children, Lord,
filled with your Spirit.
We want so much for them to develop and mature
in accordance with your will and plan for their lives.
Teach us to treat them as persons,
even while we must lovingly discipline them.
Teach us to listen to them—
their childish explosions of anger and frustration,
their doubts, fears, joys, and pains—
even to share with them our joys and frustrations,
so they may know we are all your fallible children.
Help us to truly love them,
and grant that they may feel assured of that love.

Leslie F. Brandt, 20th century

PRAYER FOR MY PARENTS

Lord,
keep my parents in your love.
Lord,
bless them and keep them.
Lord,
please let me have money and strength
and keep my parents for many more years
so that I can take care of them.

Prayer from Ghana

THE DOOR OF THIS HOUSE

O God,
make the door of this house wide enough
to receive all who need human love and fellowship;
narrow enough to shut out all envy, pride and strife.

Make its threshold smooth enough to be
no stumbling block to children,
nor to straying feet,
but rugged and strong enough
to turn back the tempter's power.
God make the door of this house the gateway
to thine eternal kingdom.

Bishop Thomas Ken, 1637-1711

THE DAY RETURNS

The day returns and brings us the petty round
of irritating concerns and duties.

Help us to play the man, help us to perform them
with laughter and kind faces.

Let cheerfulness abound with industry.
Give us to go blithely on our business all this day,
bring us to our resting beds weary and content
and undishonored,
and grant us in the end the gift of sleep.

Robert Louis Stevenson, 1850-94

YOUR TOLERANCE

For this new day of promise and possibility, Lord,
I want to praise you not only with my lips,
but with my living.

Teach me to share this day with others
in a true spirit of celebration, openness, and grace.
In every hour preserve me
from the smooth and easy answers of intolerance.
Deny to me, Father, the idle luxury
of venting my frustrations and rage
upon the usual, carefully selected scapegoats.
Help me to recognize within my own heart
all the potential for racism and bigotry,
for blind violence, brutality, and repression,
that I am so swift to point out in others.
And let me see that this inner potential finds
its most immediate, and perhaps its most destructive
expression in the scorn and contempt I reserve
for those who dare to disagree with me.
Teach me to value all with whom I spend my time
as fellow human beings,
your precious gifts to me this day.

Fill me with *your* tolerance—
no empty, undiscriminating acceptance of everything,
rather a difficult, testing tolerance,
a tolerance that combines
a basic, non-negotiable respect for all individuals,
with a self-sacrificing quest for justice and truth.

Above all, Father, fill me with the one power
that can bring people together by attraction,
and not by compulsion—the power of your love.
In that power may I spend my self
in healing, in reconciling,
in binding up this splintered world.

J. Barrie Shepherd, 20th century

PRAYER FOR AN OPEN MIND

O Lord, help me not to despise or
oppose what I do not understand.

William Penn, 1644-1718

FOR A HOLY HEART

Lord, grant me a holy heart
that sees always what is fine and pure
and is not frightened at the sight of sin,
but creates order wherever it goes.
Grant me a heart that knows nothing
of boredom, weeping and sighing.
Let me not be too concerned
with the bothersome thing I call "myself."
Lord, give me a sense of humor
and I will find happiness in life and profit for others.

St. Thomas More, 1478-1535

A STEADFAST HEART

Give me, O Lord, a steadfast heart,
which no unworthy affection may drag downwards;
give me an unconquered heart,
which no tribulation can wear out;
give me an upright heart,
which no unworthy purpose may tempt aside.
Bestow on me also, O Lord my God,
understanding to know you,
diligence to seek you,
wisdom to find you,
and a faithfulness that may finally embrace you,
through Jesus Christ our Lord, Amen.

St. Thomas Aquinas, 1225-74

LATE HAVE I LOVED THEE

Late have I loved Thee,
O Beauty so ancient and so new;
late have I loved Thee; for behold
Thou wert within me and I outside;
and I sought Thee outside
and in my unloveliness
fell upon those lovely things
that Thou hast made.
Thou wert with me
and I was not with Thee.
I was kept from Thee by those things,
yet had they not been in Thee,
they would not have been at all.
Thou didst call and cry to me
to break open my deafness:
and Thou didst send forth thy beams
and shine upon me
and chase away my blindness:
Thou didst breathe fragrance upon me,
and I drew in my breath and do now pant for Thee:
I tasted Thee, and now hunger and thirst for Thee:
Thou didst touch me,
and I have burned for Thy peace.

St. Augustine, 354-450

O LORD, SUPPORT US

O Lord,
support us all the day long,
until the shadows lengthen and the evening comes,
and the busy world is hushed
and the fever of life is over and our work is done.
Then, Lord, in your mercy,
grant us a safe lodging, and a holy rest,
and peace at the last;
through Jesus Christ our Lord.

John Henry Newman, 1801-90

FOR COURAGE

Lord Jesus, teach me to be generous;
teach me to serve you as you deserve,
to give and not to count the cost,
to fight and not to heed the wounds,
to toil and not to seek for rest,
to labor and not to seek reward,
except that of knowing that I do your will.
Amen.

St. Ignatius Loyola, 1491-1556

IN SILENCE

Father, I praise you with all these
my brothers,
and they give voice
to my own heart and to my own silence.
We are all one silence
and a diversity of voices.
You have made us together, you have made us
one and many,
you have placed me here in the midst
as witness, as awareness, and as joy.
Here I am.
In me the world is present and You are present,
and I am a link in the chain of light and presence.
You have made me a kind of center,
but a center that is nowhere. And yet
I am "here",
let us say I am "here" under these trees,
not others.
If I have any choice to make,
it is to live here and perhaps die here.
But in any case

it is not the living or dying that matters,
but speaking your name
with confidence in the light, in this unvisited place;
to speak your name "Father"
just by being here as "son"
in the Spirit and the light which you have given,
and which are no earthly light. . .
To be here
with the silence of Sonship in my heart
is to be a center
in which all things converge upon you.
That is surely enough for the time being.
Therefore, Father, I beg you
to keep me in this silence so that I may learn from it
the word of your peace
and the word of your mercy
and the word of your gentleness to the world
and that through them perhaps
your word of peace may make itself heard
where it has not been possible for anyone to hear it
for a long time.

Thomas Merton, 20th century

AUTUMN

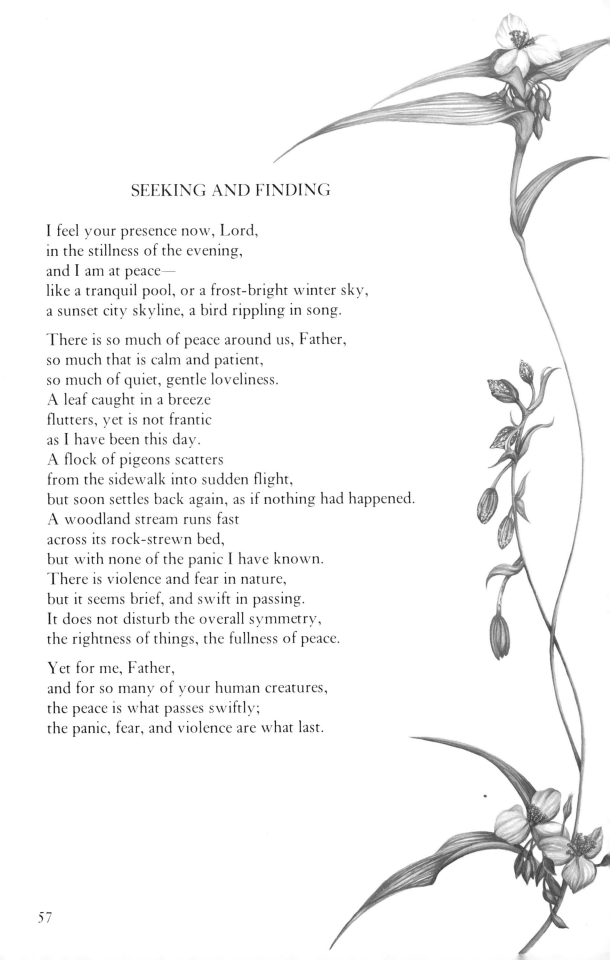

SEEKING AND FINDING

I feel your presence now, Lord,
in the stillness of the evening,
and I am at peace—
like a tranquil pool, or a frost-bright winter sky,
a sunset city skyline, a bird rippling in song.

There is so much of peace around us, Father,
so much that is calm and patient,
so much of quiet, gentle loveliness.
A leaf caught in a breeze
flutters, yet is not frantic
as I have been this day.
A flock of pigeons scatters
from the sidewalk into sudden flight,
but soon settles back again, as if nothing had happened.
A woodland stream runs fast
across its rock-strewn bed,
but with none of the panic I have known.
There is violence and fear in nature,
but it seems brief, and swift in passing.
It does not disturb the overall symmetry,
the rightness of things, the fullness of peace.

Yet for me, Father,
and for so many of your human creatures,
the peace is what passes swiftly;
the panic, fear, and violence are what last.

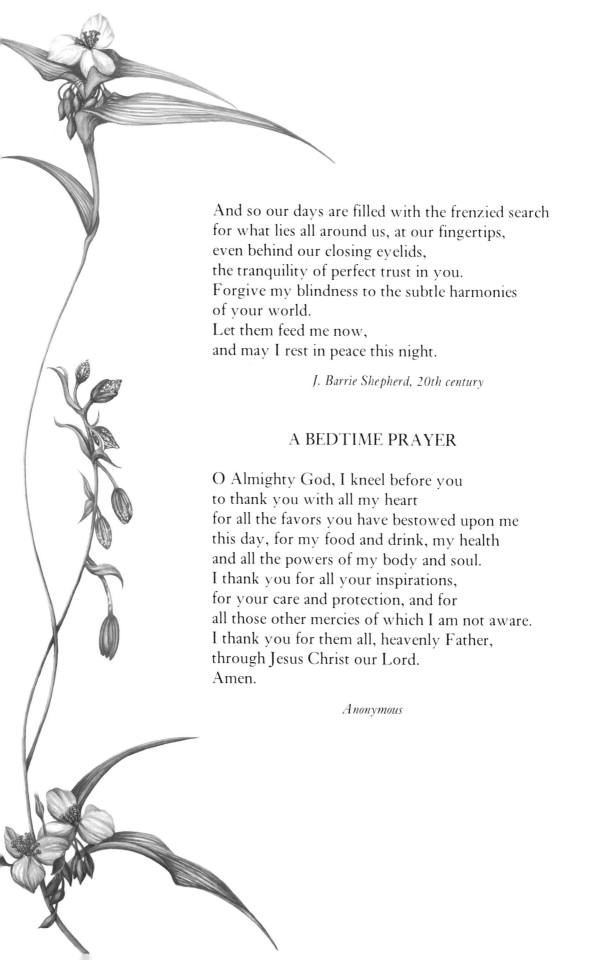

And so our days are filled with the frenzied search
for what lies all around us, at our fingertips,
even behind our closing eyelids,
the tranquility of perfect trust in you.
Forgive my blindness to the subtle harmonies
of your world.
Let them feed me now,
and may I rest in peace this night.

J. Barrie Shepherd, 20th century

A BEDTIME PRAYER

O Almighty God, I kneel before you
to thank you with all my heart
for all the favors you have bestowed upon me
this day, for my food and drink, my health
and all the powers of my body and soul.
I thank you for all your inspirations,
for your care and protection, and for
all those other mercies of which I am not aware.
I thank you for them all, heavenly Father,
through Jesus Christ our Lord.
Amen.

Anonymous

SEEKING

O my God,
how does it happen in this poor old world
that thou art so great and yet nobody finds thee,
that thou callest so loudly and yet nobody hears thee,
that thou givest thyself to everybody and yet
nobody knows thy name?
Men flee from thee and say they cannot find thee;
they turn their backs and say they cannot see thee;
they stop their ears and say they cannot hear thee.

Hans Denck, 16th century

HELP THOU MY UNBELIEF

Lord, I want to love you, yet I'm not sure.
I want to trust you, yet I'm afraid of being taken in.
I know I need you, yet I'm ashamed of the need.
I want to pray, yet I'm afraid of being a hypocrite.
I need my independence, yet I fear to be alone.
I want to belong, yet I must be myself.
Take me, Lord, yet leave me alone.
Lord, I believe; help thou my unbelief.
O Lord, if you are there, you do understand, don't you?
Give me what I need but leave me free to choose.
Help me work it out my own way, but don't let me go.
Let me understand myself, but don't let me despair.
Come unto me, O Lord—I want you there.
Lighten my darkness—but don't dazzle me.
Help me to see what I need to do and give me
strength to do it.
O Lord, I believe; help thou my unbelief.

Bernard, SSF, 20th century

HONEST GRATITUDE

Gratitude is a difficult emotion, Father.
So often I am told to thank you
for food and clothing, health and strength,
the beauty of nature, the privilege of freedom,
but I don't really feel grateful.
I go through the motions of thanks, nothing more.

Yet, when I consider,
there *are* many things for which I am thankful.
I thank you, Lord,
for moments of inspiration,
flashes of joy, glimpses of truth.
I thank you for the hidden strengths
that carry me through the stresses of each hour.
I thank you for peace and relaxation
at the close of a hard day's work,
for grace that surprises me, now and then,
in the midst of living, and transforms it for an instant,
for the comfort, and frankness, and joy
of a few real friends.
I am grateful too, Lord,
that you have not abandoned me
to my own vanity, conceit, and prejudice,
but have kept nagging away at the back of my mind
with hard choices, testing decisions,
the constant challenge in all that I do,
to find my life in losing it.

Most of all I thank you for Jesus Christ,
who opened himself to the utmost
that I might see true life in him,
fully lived out, and fully died out.
For his life risen and living in me this night,
I thank you, Father, and rejoice.

J. Barrie Shepherd, 20th century

A HEART TO LOVE THEE

Take away from me this heart of stone,
and give me a heart of flesh,
a heart to love and adore Thee,
a heart to delight in Thee,
to follow and enjoy Thee,
for Christ's sake.

St. Ambrose of Milan, 4th century

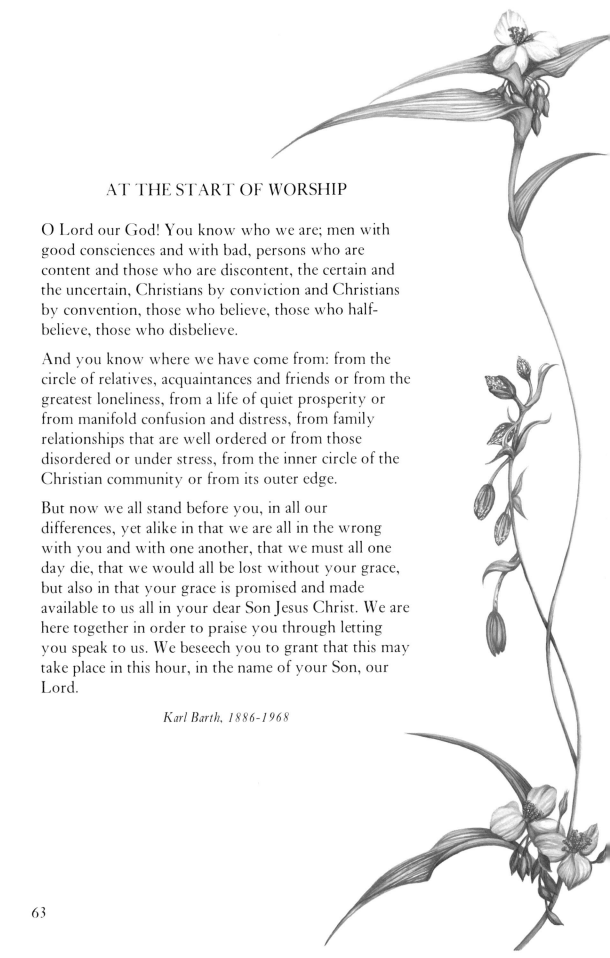

AT THE START OF WORSHIP

O Lord our God! You know who we are; men with good consciences and with bad, persons who are content and those who are discontent, the certain and the uncertain, Christians by conviction and Christians by convention, those who believe, those who half-believe, those who disbelieve.

And you know where we have come from: from the circle of relatives, acquaintances and friends or from the greatest loneliness, from a life of quiet prosperity or from manifold confusion and distress, from family relationships that are well ordered or from those disordered or under stress, from the inner circle of the Christian community or from its outer edge.

But now we all stand before you, in all our differences, yet alike in that we are all in the wrong with you and with one another, that we must all one day die, that we would all be lost without your grace, but also in that your grace is promised and made available to us all in your dear Son Jesus Christ. We are here together in order to praise you through letting you speak to us. We beseech you to grant that this may take place in this hour, in the name of your Son, our Lord.

Karl Barth, 1886-1968

A CLOSER WALK WITH GOD

O! for a closer walk with God,
A calm and heav'nly frame;
A light to shine upon the road
That leads me to the lamb!

The dearest idol I have known,
Whate'er that idol be;
Help me to tear it from thy throne,
And worship only thee.

So shall my walk be close with God,
Calm and serene my frame;
So purer light shall mark the road
That leads me to the lamb.

William Cowper, 1731-1800

RELAXING

Father, so often I fail
to find you in my praying,
despite all my best efforts.
I enter grimly into prayer,
trying to gather up all my wandering thoughts
and suppress them, control them for you.
I seek your presence, Lord,

attempting to clear my mind
of all possible distractions,
all conceivable interruptions.
Yet, no matter how I concentrate,
my thoughts thread their way back
to the business of my daily life and work.
Am I so wrong in this, Lord?
Surely if these are the things that concern me,
the matters around which my life revolves,
then they should form the content of my prayers.
When will I learn that prayers
are not times set aside from life,
reserved for thinking pure and holy thoughts,
but prayer is a life-long dialog with you
concerning all that is important in my life?

Help me now,
not to concentrate,
but rather to relax.
Convince me that I cannot raise myself
into your holy presence by sheer determination,
that you are always already here,
and all I have to do
is to open myself to your presence.
Help me
to be myself
in my praying, Lord.

J. Barrie Shepherd, 20th century

IN TIMES OF DOUBTS

In times of doubts and questionings,
when our belief is perplexed
by new learning, new teaching, new thought,
when our faith is strained by creeds, by doctrines,
by mysteries beyond our understanding,
give us the faithfulness of learners
and the courage of believers in thee;
give us boldness to examine and faith
to trust all truth;
patience and insight to master difficulties;
stability to hold fast our tradition with enlightened
interpretation,
to admit all fresh truth made known to us,
and in times of trouble,
to grasp new knowledge readily and to combine it
loyally and honestly with the old;
alike from stubborn rejection of new revelations,
and from hasty assurances
that we are wiser than our fathers,
save us and help us, we humbly beseech thee, O Lord.

Bishop George Ridding, 1828-1904

RIGHT AND MIGHT

Lord, give us faith that right makes might.

Abraham Lincoln, 1809-65

FOR OUR ENEMIES

Merciful and loving Father,
we beseech thee most humbly,
even with all our hearts,
to pour out upon our enemies with
bountiful hands,
whatsoever things thou knowest
will do them good.

16th century prayer

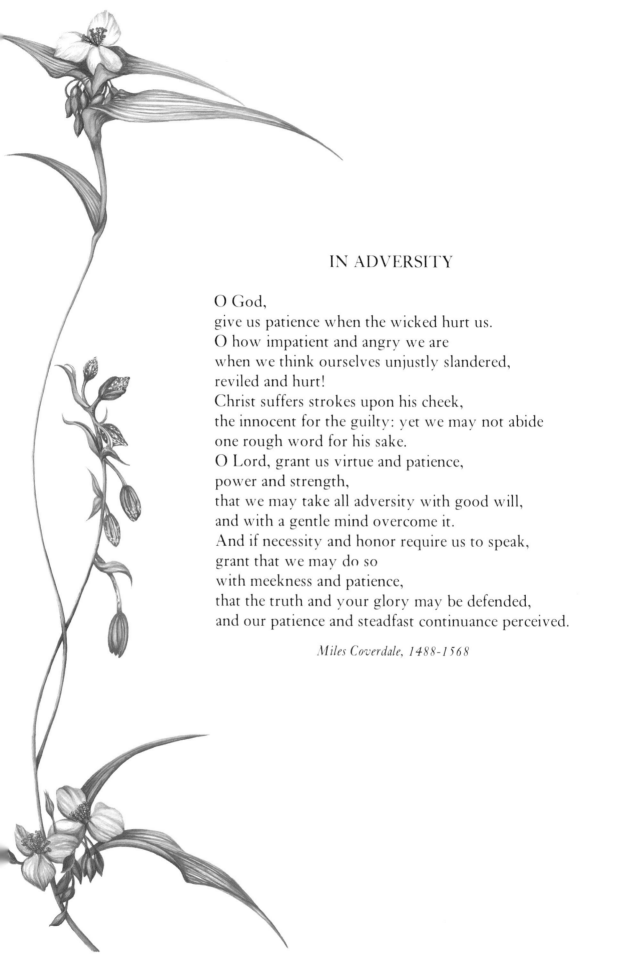

IN ADVERSITY

O God,
give us patience when the wicked hurt us.
O how impatient and angry we are
when we think ourselves unjustly slandered,
reviled and hurt!
Christ suffers strokes upon his cheek,
the innocent for the guilty: yet we may not abide
one rough word for his sake.
O Lord, grant us virtue and patience,
power and strength,
that we may take all adversity with good will,
and with a gentle mind overcome it.
And if necessity and honor require us to speak,
grant that we may do so
with meekness and patience,
that the truth and your glory may be defended,
and our patience and steadfast continuance perceived.

Miles Coverdale, 1488-1568

THE SERENITY PRAYER

God grant me the
Serenity to accept the things
I cannot change,

Courage to change the things I can, and
Wisdom to know the difference.

Living one day at a time,
Enjoying one moment at a time,
Accepting hardship as the pathway to peace,

Taking, as He did, this sinful
World as it is, not as I would have it,

Trusting that He will make all
things right if I surrender
to His Will,

That I may be reasonably happy
in this life, and supremely
happy with Him forever in the next.
Amen.

Reinhold Niebuhr, 1892-1971

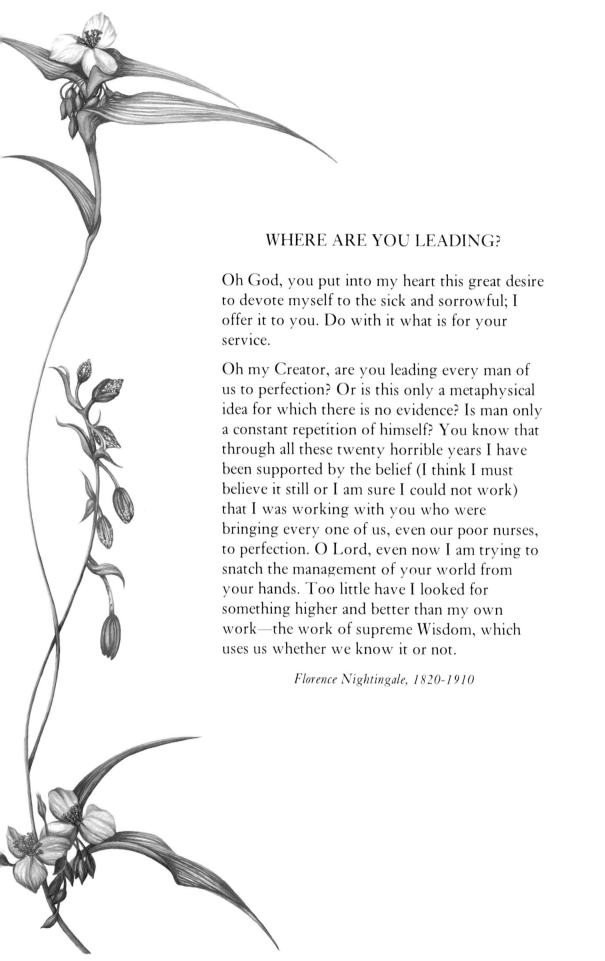

WHERE ARE YOU LEADING?

Oh God, you put into my heart this great desire to devote myself to the sick and sorrowful; I offer it to you. Do with it what is for your service.

Oh my Creator, are you leading every man of us to perfection? Or is this only a metaphysical idea for which there is no evidence? Is man only a constant repetition of himself? You know that through all these twenty horrible years I have been supported by the belief (I think I must believe it still or I am sure I could not work) that I was working with you who were bringing every one of us, even our poor nurses, to perfection. O Lord, even now I am trying to snatch the management of your world from your hands. Too little have I looked for something higher and better than my own work—the work of supreme Wisdom, which uses us whether we know it or not.

Florence Nightingale, 1820-1910

THE ROAD AHEAD

My Lord God, I have no idea where I am going.
I do not see the road ahead of me.
I cannot know for certain where it will end.
Nor do I really know myself,
and the fact that I think that I am following your will
does not mean that I am actually doing so.
But I believe that the desire to please you
does in fact please you.
And I hope I have that desire in all that I am doing.
I hope that I will never do anything
apart from that desire.
And I know that if I do this,
you will lead me by the right road
though I may know nothing about it.
Therefore will I trust you always
though I may seem to be lost
and in the shadow of death.
I will not fear, for you are ever with me,
and you will never leave me to face my perils alone.

Thomas Merton, 20th century

PRAYER FOR GOD'S HELP

O God, from whom to be turned is to fall,
to whom to be turned is to rise,
and with whom to stand is to abide for ever;
grant us in all our duties your help,
in all our perplexities your guidance,
in all our dangers your protection,
and in all our sorrows your peace,
through Jesus Christ our Lord,
Amen.

St. Augustine, 354-430

IT IS ENOUGH

As the rain hides the stars,
as the autumn mist hides the hills,
as the clouds veil the blue of the sky,
so the dark happenings of my lot
hide the shining of thy face from me.
Yet, if I may hold thy hand in the darkness,
it is enough.
Since I know that though I may stumble
in my going, thou dost not fall.

Gaelic, translated by Alistair McLean

PSALM 23

The Lord is my shepherd; I shall not want.
He maketh me to lie down in green pastures,
He leadeth me beside the still waters,
He restoreth my soul.

He leadeth me in the paths of righteousness
for his name's sake.
Yea, though I walk through the valley
of the shadow of death,
I will fear no evil, for thou art with me.
Thy rod and thy staff they comfort me.
Thou preparest a table before me
in the presence of mine enemies;
Thou anointest my head with oil,
my cup runneth over.
Surely goodness and mercy shall follow me
all the days of my life;
And I will dwell in the house of the Lord forever.

LOOKING BACK

When I look back upon my life nigh spent,
Nigh spent, although the stream as yet flows on,
I more of follies than of sins repent,
Less of offence than of Love's shortcomings moan,
With self, O Father, leave me not alone—
Leave not with the beguiler the beguiled;
Besmirched and ragged, Lord, take back thine own:
A fool I bring thee to be made a child.

George Macdonald, 1824-1905

IN PRAISE OF MATTER

Blessed be you, harsh matter,
barren soil, stubborn rock:
you who yield only to violence,
you who force us to work
if we would eat.

Blessed be you, perilous matter,
violent sea, untameable passion:
you who unless we fetter you
will devour us.

Blessed be you mighty matter,
irresistable march of evolution,
reality ever new-born:
you who by constantly shattering our
mental categories,
force us to go ever further and further
in our pursuit of the truth.

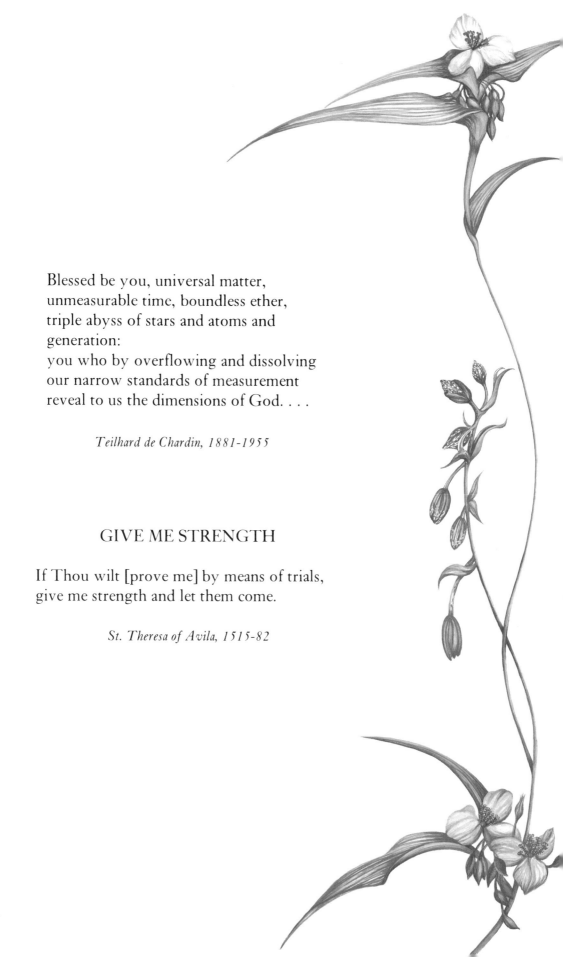

Blessed be you, universal matter,
unmeasurable time, boundless ether,
triple abyss of stars and atoms and
generation:
you who by overflowing and dissolving
our narrow standards of measurement
reveal to us the dimensions of God. . . .

Teilhard de Chardin, 1881-1955

GIVE ME STRENGTH

If Thou wilt [prove me] by means of trials,
give me strength and let them come.

St. Theresa of Avila, 1515-82

WINTER

AT THE START OF A DAY

Who can tell what a day may bring forth?
Cause me therefore, gracious God,
to live every day as if it were to be my last,
for I know not but that it may be such.
Cause me to live now as I shall wish I had done
when I come to die.
O grant that I may not die with any guilt
on my conscience,
or any known sin unrepented of,
but that I may be found in Christ,
who is my only Savior and Redeemer.

Thomas à Kempis, 1380-1471

PRAYER OF AN AGING WOMAN

Lord, you know better than I know myself that I am growing older, and will some day be old. Keep me from getting talkative, and particularly from the fatal habit of thinking that I must say something on every subject and on every occasion.

Release me from craving to straighten out everybody's affairs. Make me thoughtful, but not moody; helpful, but not bossy. With my vast store of wisdom it seems a pity not to use it all, but you know, Lord, that I want a few friends at the end. Keep my mind from the recital of endless details—give me wings to come to the point.

I ask for grace enough to listen to the tales of others' pains. But seal my lips on my own aches and pains—they are increasing, and my love of

rehearsing them is becoming sweeter as the years go by. Help me to endure them with patience.

I dare not ask for improved memory, but for a growing humility and a lessening cocksureness when my memory seems to clash with the memories of others. Teach me the glorious lesson that occasionally it is possible that I may be mistaken.

Keep me reasonably sweet. I do not want to be a saint—some of them are so hard to live with— but a sour old woman is one of the crowning works of the devil.

Give me the ability to see good things in unexpected places, and talents in unexpected people. And give me, O Lord, the grace to tell them so.

Anonymous, 17th century

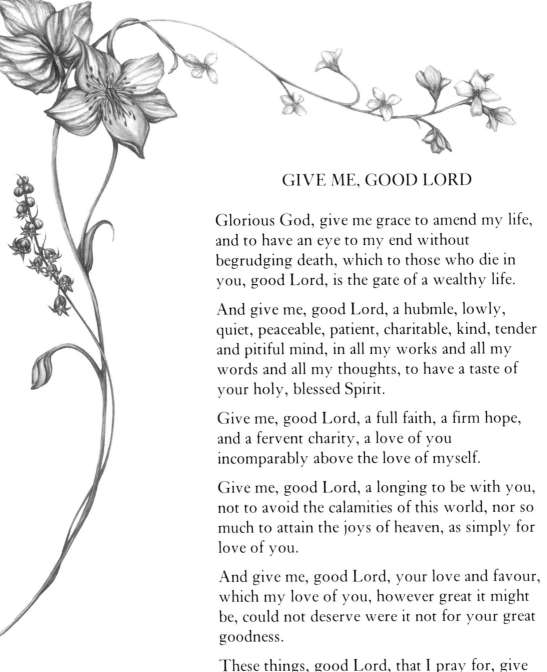

GIVE ME, GOOD LORD

Glorious God, give me grace to amend my life, and to have an eye to my end without begrudging death, which to those who die in you, good Lord, is the gate of a wealthy life.

And give me, good Lord, a hubmle, lowly, quiet, peaceable, patient, charitable, kind, tender and pitiful mind, in all my works and all my words and all my thoughts, to have a taste of your holy, blessed Spirit.

Give me, good Lord, a full faith, a firm hope, and a fervent charity, a love of you incomparably above the love of myself.

Give me, good Lord, a longing to be with you, not to avoid the calamities of this world, nor so much to attain the joys of heaven, as simply for love of you.

And give me, good Lord, your love and favour, which my love of you, however great it might be, could not deserve were it not for your great goodness.

These things, good Lord, that I pray for, give me your grace to labour for.

St. Thomas More, 1478-1535

GIVE ME A PURE HEART

Give me a pure heart—that I may see thee,
A humble heart—that I may hear thee,
A heart of love—that I may serve thee,
A heart of faith—that I may abide in thee.

To love life and men as God loves them—
for the sake of their infinite possibilities,
to wait like him
to judge like him
without passing judgment,
to obey the order when it is given
and never look back—
then he can use you—
then, perhaps, he will use you,
And if he doesn't use you—what matter.
In his hand, every moment has its meaning,
its greatness, its glory, its peace,
its co-inheritance.

Dag Hammarskjöld, 1905-61

THE ENDING AND THE BEGINNING

O Father, give the spirit power to climb
To the fountain of all light, and be purified.
Break through the mists of earth, the weight
of the clod,
Shine forth in splendour, Thou that art calm weather,
And quiet resting place for faithful souls.
To see Thee is the end and the beginning,
Thou carriest us, and Thou dost go before,
Thou art the journey, and the journey's end.

Boethius, c. 480-524

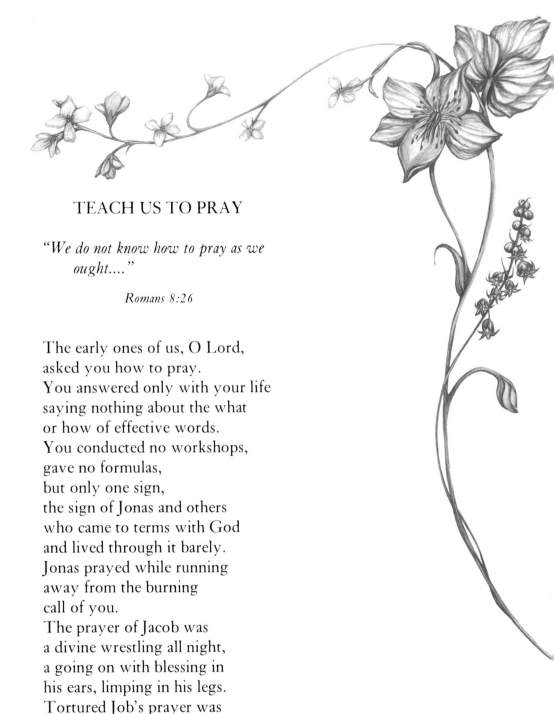

TEACH US TO PRAY

"We do not know how to pray as we ought...."

Romans 8:26

The early ones of us, O Lord,
asked you how to pray.
You answered only with your life
saying nothing about the what
or how of effective words.
You conducted no workshops,
gave no formulas,
but only one sign,
the sign of Jonas and others
who came to terms with God
and lived through it barely.
Jonas prayed while running
away from the burning
call of you.
The prayer of Jacob was
a divine wrestling all night,
a going on with blessing in
his ears, limping in his legs.
Tortured Job's prayer was
of manure, flies, cruel fate
and the theology chatter
of his preacher friends.

Prayer for Moses was the struggle
that ripped him away
from the shepherd peace
he wanted so desperately.
Jeremiah sought only a
middle-class life, a wife,
some ground to call his own.
Prayer for him was cursing
out God from jail.
Habakkuk prayed by asking
why believe in one whose
holy promise history mocks.
Paul had it out with God
over the thorn in his flesh
and all he ever got was "no."
We would learn to pray, O Lord,
yet we shrink from true
coming to terms with you.
Help us to and through
Gethscmane, be with
our wrestling, our grappling
with destiny and you.
You know well what a
horrid place is prayer.
Coax us into this holy line
of battered men who
got through to you
and found themselves.

James Carroll, 20th century

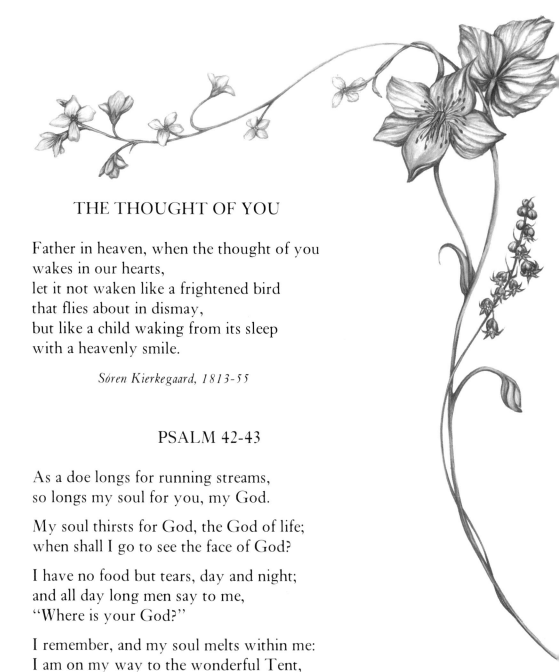

THE THOUGHT OF YOU

Father in heaven, when the thought of you
wakes in our hearts,
let it not waken like a frightened bird
that flies about in dismay,
but like a child waking from its sleep
with a heavenly smile.

Søren Kierkegaard, 1813-55

PSALM 42-43

As a doe longs for running streams,
so longs my soul for you, my God.

My soul thirsts for God, the God of life;
when shall I go to see the face of God?

I have no food but tears, day and night;
and all day long men say to me,
"Where is your God?"

I remember, and my soul melts within me:
I am on my way to the wonderful Tent,
to the house of God,
among cries of joy and praise
and an exultant throng.

Why so downcast, my soul,
why do you sigh within me?
Put your hope in God:
I shall praise him yet, my savior, my God.

When my soul is downcast within me,
I think of you;
from the land of Jordan and of Hermon,
of you, humble mountain!

Deep is calling to deep as your cataracts roar;
all your waves, your breakers,
have rolled over me.

In the daytime may Yahweh
command his love to come,
and by night may his song be on my lips,
a prayer to the God of my life!

Let me say to God, my Rock,
"Why do you forget me?
Why must I walk so mournfully,
oppressed by the enemy?"

Nearly breaking my bones my oppressors insult me,
as all day long they ask me, "Where is your God?"

Why so downcast, my soul,
why do you sigh within me?

Put your hope in God:
I shall praise him yet,
my savior, my God.

Defend me, take up my cause
against people who have no pity;
from the treacherous and cunning man
rescue me, God.

It is you, God, who are my shelter:
why do you abandon me?
Why must I walk so mournfully,
oppressed by the enemy?

Send out your light and your truth,
let these be my guide,
to lead me to your holy mountain
and to the place where you live.

Then I shall go to the altar of God,
to the God of my joy, I shall rejoice,
I shall praise you on the harp,
Lord, my God.

Why so downcast, my soul,
why do you sigh within me?
Put your hope in God: I shall praise him yet,
my savior, my God.

MORNING PRAYERS

In me there is darkness,
But with you there is light;
I am lonely, but you do not leave me;
I am feeble in heart, but with you there is help;
I am restless, but with you there is peace.
In me there is bitterness, but with you there is patience;
I do not understand your ways,
But you know the way for me.

Lord Jesus Christ,
You were poor and in distress,
a captive and forsaken as I am.
You know all man's troubles;
You abide with me when all men fail me;
You remember and seek me;
It is your will that I should know you
and turn to you.
Lord, I hear your call and follow;
Help me.

Dietrich Bonhoeffer, 1906-45

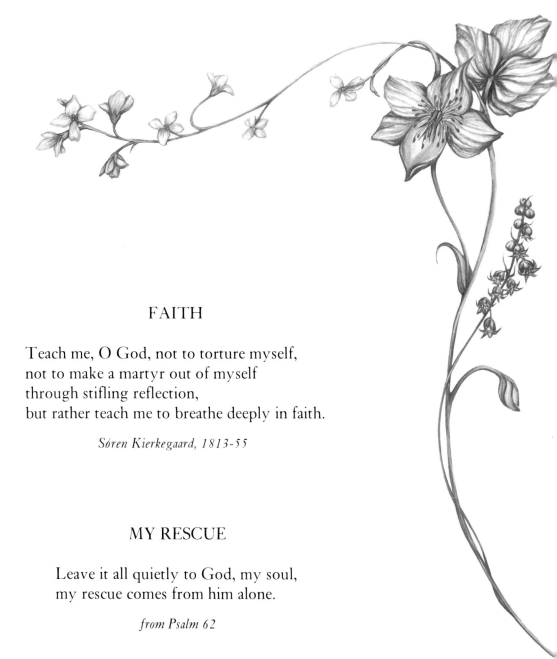

FAITH

Teach me, O God, not to torture myself,
not to make a martyr out of myself
through stifling reflection,
but rather teach me to breathe deeply in faith.

Sören Kierkegaard, 1813-55

MY RESCUE

Leave it all quietly to God, my soul,
my rescue comes from him alone.

from Psalm 62

EVENING PRAYER

Watch, dear Lord,
with those who wake, or watch, or weep tonight,
and give your angels charge over those who sleep.
Tend your sick ones, O Lord Christ,
rest your weary ones.
Bless your dying ones.
Soothe your suffering ones.
Pity your afflicted ones.
Shield your joyous ones.
And all for your love's sake.
Amen.

St. Augustine, 354-430

GO WITH US TO REST

Go with each of us to rest; if any awake,
temper to them the dark hours of watching;
and when the day returns, return to us,
our sun and comforter, and call us up
with morning faces and with morning hearts,
eager to labor, eager to be happy,
if happiness should be our portion,
and if the day be marked for sorrow,
strong to endure it.

Robert Louis Stevenson, 1850-94

PRAYER BEFORE SLEEP

I am going now into the sleep,
Be it that I in health shall wake;
If death be to me in deathly sleep,
Be it that in thine own arm's keep,
O God of grace, to new life I wake;
O be it in thy dear arm's keep,
O God of grace, that I shall awake!

from Poems of the Western Highlanders

AT OUR LAST AWAKENING

Bring us, O Lord, at our last awakening
into the house and gate of heaven,
to enter into that gate and dwell in that house,
where there shall be no darkness nor dazzling
but one equal light,
no noise nor silence, but one equal possession,
no ends or beginnings, but one equal eternity,
in the habitations of thy majesty and thy glory,
world without end.

John Donne, 1572-1631

I AM READY. . .I ACCEPT

Father,
I abandon myself into your hands;
do with me what you will.
Whatever you may do, I thank you:
I am ready for all, I accept all.
Let only your will be done in me,
and in all your creatures—
I wish no more than this, O Lord.
Into your hands I commend my soul;
I offer it to you with all the love of my heart,
for I love you, Lord, and so need to give myself,
to surrender myself into your hands without reserve,
and with boundless confidence,
for you are my Father.

Charles de Foucauld, 1858-1916

FOR THOSE WE LOVE

Lord God,
we can hope for others nothing better
than the happiness we desire for ourselves.
Therefore, I pray you, do not separate me after death
from those I have tenderly loved on earth.
Grant that where I am they may be with me,
and that I may enjoy their presence in heaven
after being so often deprived of it on earth.
Lord God, I ask you to receive your beloved children
immediately into your life-giving heart.
After this brief life on earth,
give them eternal happiness.
Amen.

St. Ambrose of Milan, 4th century

FOR THE DYING

Lord,
this night some will be gathered
to the Father.
Grant that they may go forth
surrounded by their loved ones,
without pain of body,
with clarity of mind,
and with joyful expectancy of soul.
Amen.

J. Massynberde Ford, 19th century

NIGHT IS
DRAWING NIGH

Night is drawing nigh—
For all that has been—Thanks!
For all that shall be—Yes!

Dag Hammarskjöld, 1905-61

A 'LOST LIFE'

Lord, I am willing to appear
to the world and to all
to have lost my life,
if only I may have made it good
in your sight.

Temple Gairdner, 1873-1928

TERESA'S
BOOKMARK

Let nothing disturb you;
let nothing dismay you;
all things pass:
God never changes.
Patience attains
all it strives for.
He who has God
finds he lacks nothing:
God alone suffices.

St. Teresa of Avila, 1515-82

RETURNING
SPRING

AN EGYPTIAN DOXOLOGY

May none of God's wonderful works
keep silence, night or morning.
Bright stars, high mountains, the depths of the seas,
sources of rushing rivers:
may all these break into song as we sing
to Father, Son, and Holy Spirit.
May all the angels in the heavens reply:
Amen! Amen! Amen!
Power, praise, honour, eternal glory
to God, the only Giver of grace.
Amen! Amen! Amen!

Egypt, 3rd century

PRAYER FOR THE PLANET

Here we are, Lord—a planet at prayer.
Attune our spirits that we may hear your
harmonies and bow before your creative power,
that we may face our violent discords and join
with your Energy to make heard in every heart
your hymn of peace.

Here we are, Lord—a militarized planet.
Transform our fears that we may transform our
war fields into wheat fields, arms into
handshakes, missiles into messengers of peace.

Here we are, Lord—a polluted planet.
Purify our vision that we may perceive ways to
purify our beloved lands, cleanse our precious
waters, de-smog our life-giving air.

Here we are, Lord—an exploited planet.
Heal our hearts, Lord, that we may respect our
resources, hold priceless our people, and provide
for our starving children an abundance of daily
bread.

Joan Metzner, MM, 20th century

THE GREATEST COMMANDMENTS

The first of all the commandments is,
Hear, O Israel; the Lord our God is one Lord:
And thou shalt love the Lord thy God
with all thy soul, and with all thy mind,
and with all thy strength:
this is the first commandment.
And the second is like, namely this,
Thou shalt love thy neighbor as thyself.
There is none other commandment
greater than these.

Mark 12:29-31

YOUR FAMILY

People will be born today, Lord, and people will die.
People will marry, will leave home, will return again.
People will feast, will go hungry,
will make money, steal money, give money away.
People will succeed today, beyond their wildest
dreams.
People will fail themselves into abysmal despair.
People will kill today, and people will love.

This human family, Father, is vast,
beyond all my comprehension,
beyond even my compassion.
I know it is here,
at times, I even admit to being a part of it,
but its complexity, its contrasts, as well as its sheer
size, overwhelm me.
Yet we are all your family, Lord.
Bring us closer together.

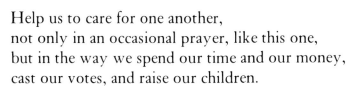

Help us to care for one another,
not only in an occasional prayer, like this one,
but in the way we spend our time and our money,
cast our votes, and raise our children.

In the way that I live this day,
may I demonstrate at least respect,
if not outright love, for all human beings.
Renew in me, Lord, the realization
that the loss of any individual diminishes me,
for we all have something to share,
something to teach, something to give.
Thus let me make the human family
less an ideal, more a reality,
in my own life,
and in the life of my own small family.
In the name of Jesus, who first taught us
to call you, "Father."

J. Barrie Shepherd, 20th century

THE BEATITUDES

Blessed are the poor in spirit:
for theirs is the kingdom of heaven.
Blessed are they that mourn:
for they shall be comforted.
Blessed are the meek:
for they shall inherit the earth.
Blessed are they which do hunger and thirst
after righteousness:
for they shall be filled.
Blessed are the merciful:
for they shall obtain mercy.
Blessed are the pure in heart:
for they shall see God.
Blessed are the peacemakers:
for they shall be called the children of God.
Blessed are they which are persecuted for
righteousness' sake:
for theirs is the kingdom of heaven.
Blessed are ye, when men shall revile you,
and persecute you,
and shall say all manner of evil against you falsely,
for my sake.
Rejoice, and be exceeding glad:
for great is your reward in heaven:
for so persecuted they the prophets
which were before you.

Matthew 5:3-12

PRAYER FOR UNITY

Savior of human suffering
to which You have given living value,
be also the Savior of human unity;
compel us to discard our pettinesses,
and to venture forth, resting upon You,
into the undaunted seas of charity.

Teilhard de Chardin, 1881-1955

107

FOR OUR RICHES

I pray today,
not only for the suffering,
the hungry, the war-torn, the lost,
for they are always in my prayers.
But I pray for the wealthy,
the prosperous, the comfortable of this world.

Open the sleepy eyes
of the wealthy nations, Lord.
Awaken us from our overfed slumber
to responsibility for our needy brothers and sisters.
Teach us, again,
how much we have that we do not need,
and how much they need that they do not have.
Persuade us,
set the conviction deep within us,
that our comfort is at their expense,
our well-being at the cost of their misery.

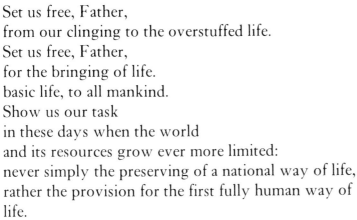

Set us free, Father,
from our clinging to the overstuffed life.
Set us free, Father,
for the bringing of life.
basic life, to all mankind.
Show us our task
in these days when the world
and its resources grow ever more limited:
never simply the preserving of a national way of life,
rather the provision for the first fully human way of
life.

May my life, Lord,
begin to witness to these truths
and to follow the path of the one
who gave his life to save our lives
and to bring life, new life, to all.

J. Barrie Shepherd, 20th century

THE HEALING GRACE OF
YOUR LOVE

Let the healing grace of your love, O Lord,
so transform me, that I may play my part
in the transfiguration of the world
from a place of suffering, death and corruption
to a realm of infinite light, joy and love.
Make me so obedient to your Spirit
that my life may become a living prayer,
and a witness to your unfailing presence.

Martin Israel, 20th century

A RUNE OF HOSPITALITY

I saw a stranger today
I put food for him in the eating-place
And drink in the drinking-place
And music in the listening-place.
In the Holy Name of the Trinity
He blessed myself and my house
My goods and my family.
And the lark said in her warble
Often, often, often
Goes Christ in the stranger's guise
O, oft and oft, and oft,
Goes Christ in the stranger's guise.

Anonymous

CHRIST'S BODY

Christ has no body now on earth but yours;
yours are the only hands with which he can do his
work,
yours are the only feet with which he can go about
the world,
yours are the only eyes through which his compassion
can shine forth upon a troubled world.
Christ has no body now on earth but yours.

St. Teresa of Avila, 1515-82

AFTER LEARNING TO READ

We are going home to many who cannot read.
So, Lord, make us to be Bibles
so that those who cannot read the Book
can read it in us.

A Chinese woman's prayer

THE WORK OF PEACE

Give us courage, O Lord, to stand up and be counted,
to stand up for those who cannot stand up for
themselves,
to stand up for ourselves when it is needful for us to do
so.
Let us fear nothing more than we fear you.
Let us love nothing more than we love you,
for thus we shall fear nothing also.
Let us have no other God before you,
whether nation or party or state or church.
Let us seek no other peace but the peace which is
yours,
and make us its instruments,
opening our eyes and our ears and our hearts,
so that we should know always what work of peace
we may do for you.

Alan Paton, 20th century

FATHER, FORGIVE

The hatred which divides nation from nation,
race from race, class from class,
Father, forgive.
The covetous desires of men and nations
to possess what is not their own,
Father, forgive.
The greed which exploits the labours of men,
and lays waste the earth,
Father, forgive.
Our envy of the welfare and happiness of others,
Father, forgive.
Our indifference to the plight of the homeless
and the refugee,
Father, forgive.
The lust which uses for ignoble ends
the bodies of men and women,
Father, forgive.
The pride which leads to trust in ourselves
and not in God,
Father, forgive.

Coventry Cathedral Prayer, 20th century

FOR A NATION AT WAR

Grant, O merciful God, that with malice
toward none, with charity to all, with firmness
in the right as thou givest us to see the right, we
may strive to finish the work we are in; to bind
up the nation's wounds; to care for him who
shall have borne the battle and for his widow
and his orphan; to do all which may achieve and
cherish a just and lasting peace among ourselves
and with all nations.

Abraham Lincoln, 1809-65

INSTRUMENT OF YOUR PEACE

Lord, make me an instrument of your peace.
Where there is hatred, let me sow love,
Where there is injury, pardon,
Where there is doubt, faith,
Where there is despair, hope,
Where there is darkness, light,
Where there is sadness, joy.

O Divine Master, grant that I may not so much seek
to be consoled as to console,
not so much to be understood as to understand,
not so much to be loved, as to love;
for it is in giving that we receive,
it is in pardoning that we are pardoned,
it is in dying, that we awake to eternal life.

St. Francis of Assisi, 1181-1226

TO BE ALL TO YOU

Sever me from myself that I may be grateful to you;
may I perish to myself that I may be safe in you;
may I die to myself that I may live in you;
may I wither to myself that I may blossom in you;
may I be emptied of myself that I may abound in you;
may I be nothing to myself that I may be all to you.

Desiderius Erasmus, 1469-1536

COME, MY WAY,
MY TRUTH, MY LIFE

Come, my Way, my Truth, my Life:
Such a Way as gives us breath:
Such a Truth as ends all strife:
Such a Life as killeth death.

Come, my Light, my Feast, my Strength:
Such a Light, as shows a feast:
Such a Feast, as mends in length:
Such a Strength, as makes his guest.

Come, my Joy, my Love, my Heart:
Such a Joy, as none can move:
Such a Love, as none can part:
Such a Heart, as joys in love.

George Herbert, 1593-1633

RESURRECTION

'Thy dead shall live, their bodies shall rise.
O dwellers in the dust, awake and sing for joy!
For thy dew is a dew of light,
and on the land of the shades thou wilt let it fall.'

Isaiah 26:19

IN THE PALM OF HIS HAND

May the road rise to meet you,
May the wind always be at your back,
May the sun shine warm upon your face,
May rains fall soft upon your field,
May God hold you in the palm of his hand.

Irish Blessing

121

SOMEDAY

Someday, after we have mastered
the winds, the waves and gravity,
we shall harness for God the energies of love.
Then, for the second time in the history
of the world,
man will have discovered fire.

Teilhard de Chardin, 1881-1955

Favorite Prayers

ACKNOWLEDGMENTS

The editors would like to thank the authors and publishers of the following works for their gracious permission to include them in *A Garden of Prayer*:

"Prayer of the Butterfly," *Prayers from the Ark* by Carmen de Gasztold. Copyright 1947, 1955 by Editions du Cloitre. English text copyright © 1962 by Rumer Godden. All rights reserved. Reprinted by permission of Viking Penguin Inc.

"The Canticle of Brother Sun" and "Instrument of Your Peace" from *St. Francis of Assisi Omnibus of Sources: Early Writings and Biographies*, edited by Marion A. Halaig. By permission of Franciscan World Press.

"Native American Prayer," "In Silence" by Thomas Merton, "Evening Prayer" by St. Augustine, and "Prayer for the Planet" by Joan Metzner, all excerpted from *Pocketbook of Prayers* by Basil Pennington, O.C.S.O. Copyright © 1986 by Cistercian Abbey of Spencer, Inc. Reprinted by permission of Doubleday, a division of Bantam, Doubleday, Dell Publishing Group, Inc.

"The Wish of Machán Liath," and "Christ's Bounties" by Tadhg Og O'Huiginn, from *A Celtic Missionary* by Kenneth H. Jackson. Reprinted by permission of Routledge and Kegan Paul, Associated Book Publishers (UK), Ltd.

"With Me, Lord," "Your Tolerance," "Seeking and Finding." "Honest Gratitude," "Easing Pressure," "Relaxing," and "Your Family" from *Diary of Daily Prayer* by J. Barrie Shepherd. Reprinted by permission, copyright © Augsburg Publishing House.